P9-CDE-777

The American Red Cross

The American Red Cross

Patrick Gilbo

CHELSEA HOUSE PUBLISHERS
New York • New Haven • Philadelphia

KG5-002087

Library of Congress Cataloging-in-Publication Data

Gilbo, Patrick.
   The American Red Cross.
   (Know your government)
   Bibliography: p. 89
   Includes index.
   1. American Red Cross—History. I. Title.
II. Series: Know your government (New York, N.Y.)
HV577.G54   1987   361.7′634′0973   86-30998

ISBN 0-87754-827-7

Project Editor: Nancy Priff
Book Editor: Rafaela Ellis
Art Director: Maureen McCafferty
Series Designer: Anita Noble
Chief Copy Editor: Melissa R. Padovani
Project Coordinator: Kathleen P. Luczak
Production Manager: Brian Shulik

ABOUT THE COVER

The services provided by the American Red Cross have always reflected its
commitment to the well-being of people all over the world. Some of those
services have included (clockwise from top left) disaster relief, provision of
clothing and food to refugees, swimming instruction, and war relief efforts,
such as the preparation of medical materials.

CONTENTS

KNOW YOUR GOVERNMENT

The American Red Cross
The Bureau of Indian Affairs
The Centers for Disease Control
The Central Intelligence Agency
The Children, Youth, and
  Families Division
The Department of Agriculture
The Department of the Air Force
The Department of the Army
The Department of Commerce
The Department of Defense
The Department of Education
The Department of Energy
The Department of Health
  and Human Services
The Department of Housing
  and Urban Development
The Department of the Interior
The Department of Justice
The Department of Labor
The Department of the Navy
The Department of State
The Department of
  Transportation
The Department of the Treasury
The Drug Enforcement
  Administration
The Environmental
  Protection Agency
The Equal Opportunities
  Commission
The Federal Aviation
  Administration
The Federal Bureau of
  Investigation
The Federal Communications
  Commission
The Federal Election Commission

The Federal Railroad
  Administration
The Food and Drug
  Administration
The Food and Nutrition Division
The House of Representatives
The Immigration and
  Naturalization Service
The Internal Revenue Service
The Interstate Commerce
  Commission
The National Foundation on the
  Arts and Humanities
The National Park Service
The National Science Foundation
The Presidency
The Securities and
  Exchange Commission
The Selective Service System
The Senate
The Small Business
  Administration
The Smithsonian
The Supreme Court
The Tennessee Valley Authority
The U.S. Information Agency
The U.S. Arms Control and
  Disarmament Agency
The U.S. Coast Guard
The U.S. Commission on
  Civil Rights
The U.S. Fish and Wildlife Service
The U.S. Mint
The U.S. Nuclear Regulatory
  Commission
The U.S. Postal Service
The U.S. Secret Service
The Veterans Administration

INTRODUCTION

Government: Crises of Confidence

Arthur M. Schlesinger, jr.

From the start, Americans have regarded their government with a mixture of reliance and mistrust. The men who founded the republic did not doubt the indispensability of government. "If men were angels," observed the 51st Federalist Paper, "no government would be necessary." But men are not angels. Since human beings are subject to wicked as well as to noble impulses, government was deemed essential to assure freedom and order.

At the same time, the American revolutionaries knew that government could also become a source of injury and oppression. The men who gathered in Philadelphia in 1787 to write the Constitution therefore had two purposes in mind. They wanted to establish a strong central authority and to limit that central authority's capacity to abuse its power.

To prevent the abuse of power, the founding fathers wrote two basic principles into the new Constitution. The principle of federalism divided power between the state governments and the central authority. The principle of the separation of powers subdivided the central authority itself into three branches—the executive, the legislative, and the judiciary—so that "each may be a check on the other." The *Know Your Government* series focuses on the major executive departments and agencies in these branches of the federal government.

The Constitution did not plan the executive branch in any detail. After vesting the executive power in the president, it assumed the existence of "executive departments" without specifying what these departments should be. Congress began defining their functions in 1789 by creating the Departments of State, Treasury, and War. The secretaries in charge of these departments made up President Washington's first cabinet. Congress also provided for a legal officer, and President Washington soon invited the attorney general, as he was called, to attend cabinet meetings. As need required, Congress created more executive departments.

Setting up the cabinet was only the first step in organizing the American state. With almost no guidance from the Constitution, President Washington, seconded by Alexander Hamilton, his brilliant secretary of the treasury, equipped the infant republic with a working administrative structure. The Federalists believed in both executive energy and executive accountability and set high standards for public appointments. The Jeffersonian opposition had less faith in strong government and preferred local government to the central authority. But when Jefferson himself became president in 1801, although he set out to change the direction of policy, he found no reason to alter the framework the Federalists had erected.

By 1801 there were about 3,000 federal civilian employees in a nation of a little more than 5 million people. Growth in territory and population steadily enlarged national responsibilities. Thirty years later, when Jackson was president, there were more than 11,000 government workers in a nation of 13 million.

The federal establishment was increasing at a faster rate than the population.

Jackson's presidency brought significant changes in the federal service. He believed that the executive branch contained too many officials who saw their jobs as "species of property" and as "a means of promoting individual interest." Against the idea of a permanent service based on life tenure, Jackson argued for the periodic redistribution of federal offices, contending that this was the democratic way and that official duties could be made "so plain and simple that men of intelligence may readily qualify themselves for their performance." He called this policy rotation-in-office. His opponents called it the spoils system.

In fact, partisan legend exaggerated the extent of Jackson's removals. More than 80 percent of federal officeholders retained their jobs. Jackson discharged no larger a proportion of government workers than Jefferson had done a generation earlier. But the rise in these years of mass political parties gave federal patronage new importance as a means of building the party and of rewarding activists. Jackson's successors were less restrained in the distribution of spoils. As the federal establishment grew—to nearly 40,000 by 1861—the politicization of the public service excited increasing concern.

After the Civil War the spoils system became a major political issue. High-minded men condemned it as the root of all political evil. The spoilsmen, said the British commentator James Bryce, "have distorted and depraved the mechanism of politics." Patronage, by giving jobs to unqualified, incompetent, and dishonest persons, lowered the standards of public service and nourished corrupt political machines. Office-seekers pursued presidents and cabinet secretaries without mercy. "Patronage," said Ulysses S. Grant after his presidency, "is the bane of the presidential office." "Every time I appoint someone to office," said another political leader, "I make a hundred enemies

9

and one ingrate." George William Curtis, the president of the National Civil Service Reform League, summed up the indictment. He said,

> The theory which perverts public trusts into party spoils, making public employment dependent upon personal favor and not on proved merit, necessarily ruins the self-respect of public employees, destroys the function of party in a republic, prostitutes elections into a desperate strife for personal profit, and degrades the national character by lowering the moral tone and standard of the country.

The object of civil service reform was to promote efficiency and honesty in the public service and to bring about the ethical regeneration of public life. Over bitter opposition from politicians, the reformers in 1883 passed the Pendleton Act, establishing a bipartisan Civil Service Commission, competitive examinations, and appointment on merit. The Pendleton Act also gave the president authority to extend by executive order the number of "classified" jobs—that is, jobs subject to the merit system. The act applied initially only to about 14,000 of the more than 100,000 federal positions. But by the end of the 19th century 40 percent of federal jobs had moved into the classified category.

Civil service reform was in part a response to the growing complexity of American life. As society grew more organized and problems more technical, official duties were no longer so plain and simple that any person of intelligence could perform them. In public service, as in other areas, the all-round man was yielding ground to the expert, the amateur to the professional. The excesses of the spoils system thus provoked the counter-ideal of scientific public administration, separate from politics and, as far as possible, insulated against it.

The cult of the expert, however, had its own excesses. The idea that administration could be divorced from policy was an illusion. And in the realm of policy, the expert, however much segregated from partisan politics, can never attain perfect objectivity. He remains the prisoner of his own set of values. It is these values rather than technical expertise that determine fundamental judgments of public policy. To turn over such judgments to experts, moreover, would be to abandon democracy itself; for in a democracy final decisions must be made by the people and their elected representatives. "The business of the expert," the British political scientist Harold Laski rightly said, "is to be on tap and not on top."

Politics, however, were deeply ingrained in American folkways. This meant intermittent tension between the presidential government, elected every four years by the people, and the permanent government, which saw presidents come and go while it went on forever. Sometimes the permanent government knew better than its political masters; sometimes it opposed or sabotaged valuable new initiatives. In the end a strong president with effective cabinet secretaries could make the permanent government responsive to presidential purpose, but it was often an exasperating struggle.

The struggle within the executive branch was less important, however, than the growing impatience with bureaucracy in society as a whole. The 20th century saw a considerable expansion of the federal establishment. The Great Depression and the New Deal led the national government to take on a variety of new responsibilities. The New Deal extended the federal regulatory apparatus. By 1940, in a nation of 130 million people, the number of federal workers for the first time passed the 1 million mark. The Second World War brought federal civilian employment to 3.8 million in 1945. With peace, the federal establishment declined to around 2 million by 1950. Then growth resumed, reaching 2.8 million by the 1980s.

The New Deal years saw rising criticism of "big government" and "bureaucracy." Businessmen resented federal regulation. Conservatives worried about the impact of paternalistic government on individual self-reliance, on community responsibility, and on economic and personal freedom. The nation in effect renewed the old debate between Hamilton and Jefferson in the early republic, although with an ironic exchange of positions. For the Hamiltonian constituency, the "rich and well-born," once the advocate of affirmative government, now condemned government intervention, while the Jeffersonian constituency, the plain people, once the advocate of a weak central government and of states' rights, now favored government intervention.

In the 1980s, with the presidency of Ronald Reagan, the debate has burst out with unusual intensity. According to conservatives, government intervention abridges liberty, stifles enterprise, and is inefficient, wasteful, and arbitrary. It disturbs the harmony of the self-adjusting market and creates worse troubles than it solves. Get government off our backs, according to the popular cliché, and our problems will solve themselves. When government is necessary, let it be at the local level, close to the people. Above all, stop the inexorable growth of the federal government.

In fact, for all the talk about the "swollen" and "bloated" bureaucracy, the federal establishment has not been growing as inexorably as many Americans seem to believe. In 1949, it consisted of 2.1 million people. Thirty years later, while the country had grown by 70 million, the federal force had grown only by 750,000. Federal workers were a smaller percentage of the population in 1985 than they were in 1955—or in 1940. The federal establishment, in short, has not kept pace with population growth. Moreover, national defense and the postal service account for 60 percent of federal employment.

Why then the widespread idea about the remorseless growth of government? It is partly because in the 1960s the national government assumed new and intrusive functions:

12

affirmative action in civil rights, environmental protection, safety and health in the workplace, community organization, legal aid to the poor. Although this enlargement of the federal regulatory role was accompanied by marked growth in the size of government on all levels, the expansion has taken place primarily in state and local government. Whereas the federal force increased by only 27 percent in the 30 years after 1950, the state and local government force increased by an astonishing 212 percent.

Despite the statistics, the conviction flourishes in some minds that the national government is a steadily growing behemoth swallowing up the liberties of the people. The foes of Washington prefer local government, feeling it is closer to the people and therefore allegedly more responsive to popular needs. Obviously there is a great deal to be said for settling local questions locally. But local government is characteristically the government of the locally powerful. Historically, the way the locally powerless have won their human and constitutional rights has often been through appeal to the national government. The national government has vindicated racial justice against local bigotry, defended the Bill of Rights against local vigilantism, and protected natural resources against local greed. It has civilized industry and secured the rights of labor organizations. Had the states' rights creed prevailed, there would perhaps still be slavery in the United States.

The national authority, far from diminishing the individual, has given most Americans more personal dignity and liberty than ever before. The individual freedoms destroyed by the increase in national authority have been in the main the freedom to deny black Americans their rights as citizens; the freedom to put small children to work in mills and immigrants in sweatshops; the freedom to pay starvation wages, require barbarous working hours, and permit squalid working conditions; the freedom to deceive in the sale of goods and securities; the freedom to pollute the environment—all freedoms that, one supposes, a civilized nation can readily do without.

"Statements are made," said President John F. Kennedy in 1963, "labelling the Federal Government an outsider, an intruder, an adversary. . . . The United States Government is not a stranger or not an enemy. It is the people of fifty states joining in a national effort. . . . Only a great national effort by a great people working together can explore the mysteries of space, harvest the products at the bottom of the ocean, and mobilize the human, natural, and material resources of our lands."

So an old debate continues. However, Americans are of two minds. When pollsters ask large, spacious questions—Do you think government has become too involved in your lives? Do you think government should stop regulating business?—a sizable majority opposes big government. But when asked specific questions about the practical work of government—Do you favor social security? unemployment compensation? Medicare? health and safety standards in factories? environmental protection? government guarantee of jobs for everyone seeking employment? price and wage controls when inflation threatens?—a sizable majority approves of intervention.

In general, Americans do not want less government. What they want is more efficient government. They want government to do a better job. For a time in the 1970s, with Vietnam and Watergate, Americans lost confidence in the national government. In 1964, more than three-quarters of those polled had thought the national government could be trusted to do right most of the time. By 1980 only one-quarter was prepared to offer such trust. But by 1984 trust in the federal government to manage national affairs had climbed back to 45 percent.

Bureaucracy is a term of abuse. But it is impossible to run any large organization, whether public or private, without a bureaucracy's division of labor and hierarchy of authority. And

14

we live in a world of large organizations. Without bureaucracy modern society would collapse. The problem is not to abolish bureaucracy, but to make it flexible, efficient, and capable of innovation.

Two hundred years after the drafting of the Constitution, Americans still regard government with a mixture of reliance and mistrust—a good combination. Mistrust is the best way to keep government reliable. Informed criticism is the means of correcting governmental inefficiency, incompetence, and arbitrariness; that is, of best enabling government to play its essential role. For without government, we cannot attain the goals of the founding fathers. Without an understanding of government, we cannot have the informed criticism that makes government do the job right. It is the duty of every American citizen to *Know Your Government*—which is what this series is all about.

Red Cross volunteers often provide disaster relief. This one comforted a child after a large apartment fire.

ONE

A Beacon of Hope

Victims of natural disasters, wars, and other catastrophes often see the symbol of the American Red Cross—a red cross on a white background—as a beacon of hope. To disaster victims in the United States, the agency provides free assistance. To those who are starving in foreign countries, the American Red Cross offers food and other forms of aid as a member of the League of Red Cross societies. To members of America's armed forces, it provides morale-boosting services, especially in times of war. The American Red Cross also ranks as a leader in the nursing, health, and safety fields. But perhaps it is best known as the nation's foremost blood collection agency, obtaining nearly half of all the blood donated in America today.

The American Red Cross provides an opportunity for people to make the world a better place. Nearly ten million volunteers participate, including blood donors and young adults. Most are members of the more than 2,900 American Red Cross chapters providing assistance to American communities.

The Red Cross movement actually consists of three distinct groups. The first, the International Committee of the Red Cross, is an all-Swiss group. It guards the principles of the Red Cross, recognizes new national societies, and works with national governments to guide their wartime activities according to the Geneva Conventions. (The conventions recognize the Red Cross as a sign of neutrality and protect war victims, medical personnel, and equipment.) The second group, the League of Red Cross and Red Crescent Societies, was formed in 1919. It is a federation of 137 national societies—including the American Red Cross—that agree to provide mutual aid when needed. National societies make up the third group. Each national society is independent, has its own goals, and may or may not join the league. Although the American Red Cross is a member of the league, it differs from other Red Cross organizations in its concern for the morale of active soldiers, as well as sick and wounded ones, in wartime and during periods of peace.

In 1881, this volunteer, nonprofit agency was founded as a private organization. Today, the American Red Cross is a semigovernmental organization. It has a congressional charter that requires it to assist members of the armed forces, to conduct disaster relief, to run disaster preparedness programs, and to perform other services that help the government fulfull the terms of the Geneva Conventions. But the workers and funds for the agency come from the American people in the form of volunteers and contributions.

To ensure that contributions are spent for the public good, the Department of the Army checks Red Cross accounting records each year. Congress also reviews the organization's financial information and the annual report that describes its accomplishments. And the Red Cross's accomplishments—and symbol—are familiar to people everywhere.

The Red Cross symbol (and the Red Crescent used by societies in Muslim countries) signifies neutrality, as it has since

This 1927 cartoon illustrates the agency's importance to flood victims, which continues today.

1864, when it first appeared on the battlefields of the Prussian-Danish war. Because the symbol indicates a neutral status, armed forces usually won't fire at or threaten Red Cross workers. This allows them to carry out their missions in the midst of major battles. The Red Cross symbol appears on ambulances, hospitals, army tents containing mobile hospital units, and of course, on Red Cross buildings and flags around the world. Almost everyone has seen the symbol on television news broadcasts after such events as floods, earthquakes, and terrorist bombings.

The policy of neutrality also permits the Red Cross to take nonpolitical stands in world events. The organization serves all people regardless of their politics, creed, or color. If the Red Cross only helped those who held certain beliefs, its humanitarian mission would be threatened and its volunteers would be endangered when working in war-devastated areas. To the Red Cross, people come first and politics last.

Jean-Henry Dunant, a Swiss businessman, founded the Red Cross movement to provide care for soldiers wounded in battle.

TWO

The Red Cross Movement

The International Red Cross movement was founded by Jean-Henry Dunant (1828–1910), a Swiss businessman and philanthropist whose concern for humanity often moved him to action. As a young man, Dunant struggled to improve the conditions of the poor in Switzerland, worked with an organization that brought Christians and Jews together, and promoted the World Alliance of Young Men's Christian Associations (YMCAs).

In the summer of 1859, Dunant had an experience that planted the idea of the Red Cross in his mind. At that time, France and Austria were at war over Italy, which was then a collection of small states. Warfare escalated until French and Austrian troops clashed at the Battle of Solferino in Italy, which Dunant witnessed from a nearby town. "On that memorable twenty-fourth of June," he later wrote, "more than 300,000 men stood facing each other; the battle line was five leagues long, and the fighting continued for more than fifteen hours." When the smoke cleared, 39,000 dead and dying bodies littered the battlefield. The wounded were left to fend for themselves, which was the custom of the time.

For the next three days, Dunant did everything he could to help the men who lay dying. He sought the aid of doctors traveling through the area and organized a group of women from a nearby village to help him tend the wounded. Dunant and his helpers

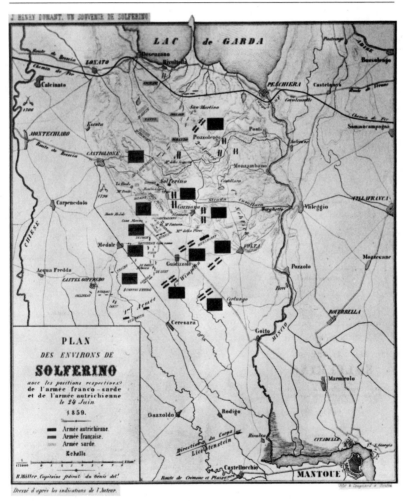

Jean-Henry Dunant's book featured this map of the Solferino battlefield in Italy, where thousands died.

brought water, offered kind words, and moved as many wounded as possible out of the hot sun and onto straw pallets in the shade.

Appalled by the battle's carnage, Dunant wondered what he could do to prevent the suffering that wars brought to young soldiers. When he returned to Switzerland, he put his feelings into words. The result was a short book published in 1862; *Un Souvenir de Solferino* (A memory of Solferino) turned the tragedy of war into a victory for humanity.

In his book, Dunant proposed the formation of volunteer societies to aid the wounded on the world's battlefields. He reflected on the efforts of the English nurse Florence Nightingale and her sister volunteers, who brought comfort to the wounded and dying in the Crimean War of 1853 to 1856. Remembering how his relief efforts had fallen short because of a lack of help and organization, Dunant wrote the following about Solferino:

> If there had been enough assistance to collect the wounded in the plains . . . there would never have been the terrible possibility of what only too probably happened the next day—living men being buried among the dead.

Dunant's straightforward accounts of the battle's brutality touched many hearts. In Europe, where war was usually glamorized, his book moved royalty and commoner alike. Influential people invited Dunant to their offices and listened to him attentively. The courts of Prussia, Austria, France, and Russia, among others, enthusiastically endorsed his idea of aiding the wounded.

Although Dunant made the world aware of the need for a relief organization, a more practical man, Gustave Moynier, turned Dunant's ideas into reality. Moynier, the president of the Geneva Public Welfare Society, realized that these ideas needed a strong international organization to carry them out.

Moynier asked Dunant, two Swiss doctors, and a Swiss army general to join him in forming a committee to accomplish this. As

Moynier gave form to Dunant's ideas by founding the International Committee of the Red Cross.

they began to organize their work, the committee members struggled to find a symbol that would identify their new relief organization readily. Eventually they selected a red cross on a white background—the reversed colors of the Swiss flag. They felt this symbol was appropriate for a relief organization formed in Switzerland. On February 17, 1863, the five members formed the International Committee of the Red Cross, which laid the foundation for the world's Red Cross and Red Crescent societies.

After much discussion, the five members realized that they couldn't bring about wide acceptance of their battlefield relief plans by themselves. So in October of 1863 they invited doctors and government officials from various countries to discuss their plans at an international conference in Geneva. Much to the committee's surprise, delegates from 16 nations responded to the call. They represented Austria, Baden, Bavaria, France, Great Britain, Hanover, Hesse, Italy, the Netherlands, Prussia, Russia, Saxony, Spain, Sweden, Switzerland, and Würtemberg.

During the conference, the representatives agreed to form a loose confederation of private relief societies that would tend the wounded and work with army medical sections in times of war.

And the tiny nation of Würtemberg established the world's first official Red Cross society.

At a later meeting, the committee and the international representatives decided that to protect against hostile fire, the Red Cross emblem should appear on ambulance wagons and hospitals as well as on armbands worn by volunteers. The principle of honoring the Red Cross emblem passed its first battlefield test in southern Denmark in February, 1864. Dr. Louis Appia, one of the original committee members, wore an armband during the Prussian-Danish War. He reported that it allowed him to move freely on the battlefield as he performed relief work.

The International Red Cross took another step to promote battlefield relief when it arranged the Geneva Convention of 1864. On August 22, representatives from 12 nations met in Switzerland to sign the first Geneva Convention treaty, the world's first significant attempt to minimize the effects of war. By signing the treaty, these nations agreed to care for sick and wounded combatants impartially; to spare medical personnel, buildings, and vehicles; and to use the red cross on medical personnel and equipment covered by the treaty. Representatives from other interested nations attended the convention but did not sign the treaty. The United States, in particular, was reluctant to sign because it viewed the treaty as an "entangling alliance" with foreign nations, which national policy prohibited.

Later Geneva Convention treaties would add to the mission of the first. They would require the signers to aid people who were wounded, sick, or shipwrecked at sea; prisoners captured by warring armies; and civilians affected by warfare. But in 1864, the treaty simply protected the armed forces' wounded and sick on the battlefield and those who cared for them.

Clara Barton founded the American Red Cross after reading Dunant's book and working with Switzerland's Red Cross.

THREE

The Birth of
the Agency

Clara Barton, the founder of the American Red Cross, became famous as a Civil War lecturer. She traveled around the country and told listeners about the horrors she had seen as a volunteer nurse on the battlefield. Her stories were so realistic and moving that Civil War veterans would stand up and cheer with tears in their eyes. Lecturing and writing took a toll on Barton's health, however, and in 1869 her doctor ordered her to take a long rest in Europe.

Barton's stay in Geneva, Switzerland, brought her in contact with the International Red Cross. She read Dunant's book about the Battle of Solferino, and Red Cross officials visited with her. The officials wanted to know why the United States had not yet signed the Geneva Convention treaty, which would enable America to have a viable Red Cross society. Barton couldn't understand why the United States would not want to help those who suffered on the battlefield. But she told the officials that the American people knew nothing about the Red Cross—that some government official had probably made the decision and nobody had challenged it.

Several months later, when France declared war on Prussia, Barton volunteered to assist the Red Cross at Basel, Switzerland, where she helped make bandages. She later worked with the Red Cross at Strasbourg, France, primarily helping civilian war victims.

Barton was deeply impressed with the Red Cross. Her work with this organization in Europe had convinced her of the need for a Red Cross in the United States, and she hoped to start one when she returned in 1873. Unfortunately, she was physically exhausted and unable to make her dream a reality until several years later.

In 1877, while recovering from exhaustion in a sanatorium in Dansville, New York, Barton heard about the outbreak of the Russo-Turkish War. The thought of war-related suffering again

As a Red Cross volunteer, Barton aided the besieged French during the Franco-Prussian War, illustrated above.

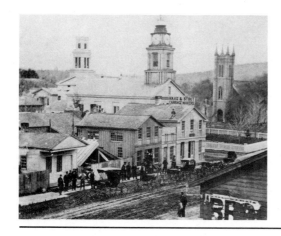

Dansville, New York, housed one of the first Red Cross chapters in America.

moved her to action. She wrote to Red Cross officials in Geneva that she felt well enough to work toward getting the United States government to sign the Geneva Convention treaty for protection of the wounded.

But government officials were suspicious of Barton's attempts to establish an American Red Cross to aid the wounded. They still viewed the signing of the Geneva Convention treaty, despite its good intentions, as an entangling alliance with foreign nations. Barton repeatedly approached government officials and repeatedly faced rejection. Determined to forge ahead instead of waiting for the United States to sign the treaty, Barton formed the American Association of the Red Cross on May 21, 1881. This private, volunteer organization soon had chapters in Dansville, Rochester, and Syracuse, New York.

Finally, President Chester A. Arthur signed the Geneva Convention treaty on March 1, 1882. The Senate ratified it on March 16, making the United States the 32d nation to agree to care for sick and wounded combatants and to use the Red Cross emblem as a symbol of neutrality. The president's signature on the treaty meant that the American Red Cross would have the government's sympathy and protection and that it could perform battlefield relief in relative safety.

The Barton Years

Barton took the Red Cross beyond the battlefield in her quest to aid the unfortunate. Although Dunant had hoped that the Red Cross could help the victims of natural disasters and other catastrophes, his main concern was helping the wounded in wartime. Barton also saw a role for the Red Cross in peace, but unlike Dunant, she did more than think about it—she made it happen.

In the summer of 1881, Barton sent food, relief supplies, and her personal agent to Michigan to help the victims of forest fires that had scarred the eastern part of the state. By helping these disaster victims, Barton's organization did what no other Red Cross society had done and went beyond the agency's original mission.

Fire and famine swept Michigan in 1881, inspiring this etching and Barton's relief efforts.

Steamboats carried Red Cross supplies to flood victims.

After the Michigan fires of 1881, the American Red Cross aided victims of a major disaster or calamity almost every year. When the Ohio and Mississippi rivers flooded in 1882 and 1884, the Red Cross was there. Steamboats flying the Red Cross flag sailed the rivers, as Barton and her assistants helped stranded victims who had lost everything. As they handed out food, clothing, blankets, and other necessities, the volunteers were rewarded by seeing the suprised faces of people who had never received this kind of help before.

The Red Cross swung into action for another flood relief operation on May 31, 1889, when a dam burst at Johnstown,

In 1889, flood waters virtually destroyed Johnstown. The Red Cross funded large-scale rebuilding after the disaster.

Pennsylvania. The water rushed in, killing hundreds of people and sweeping away thousands of homes. To shelter and care for the homeless, the agency built hotel-like structures funded by public contributions. For the first time, Red Cross work went beyond emergency assistance and into large-scale rehabilitation following a disaster.

In 1892, famine threatened Russia. With strong support from the American public, Barton sent Red Cross volunteers and supplies overseas to provide relief to starving Russians. The agency sent 500 boxcars of midwestern corn and grain aboard the chartered ship *Tynehead*.

In 1893, Barton's organization reincorporated and changed its name to the American National Red Cross—the name that it would use commonly until 1978. Barton believed that this "would make a . . . distinction between the national body and the various societies which must eventually form to work in conjunction with it." Although its name had changed, the organization continued to provide relief to those who were suffering throughout the world. In that year, the agency responded to the devastating effects of a hurricane that hit the Sea Islands off the South Carolina coast. It fed more than 30,000 starving, homeless people and gave them medical help and other forms of assistance for several months.

Civilian relief work continued, and the Red Cross engaged in its second overseas mission. In 1895, Barton sent doctors and nurses to help refugees fleeing from Armenia, where the Turks had massacred Christians. Various church groups provided the money Barton needed to send the relief team on this mission,

Red Cross funds built six hotels like the one above to house people left homeless by the Johnstown flood.

Under the Geneva Convention, Red Cross nurses sailed to Cuba to aid American soldiers during the Spanish-American War.

which used camels and outpost stations to bring the Armenians food and medical help. Barton herself directed operations from Constantinople, Turkey, in 1896.

For nearly a year before the Spanish-American War broke out in 1898, Red Cross volunteers went to Cuba to nurse and feed the Cuban rebels who were being held in prisons by the ruling Spanish troops. When war was declared on April 21, Barton formally offered the services of the American Red Cross to the United States Armed Forces, in accordance with the Geneva Convention treaty.

During the war, many people learned about the work of the Red Cross. Colonel Theodore Roosevelt—a future United States president—stopped at Barton's Red Cross camp in Cuba to buy food and supplies for his Rough Rider troops. When Barton told Roosevelt that he could not buy these items from the Red Cross "even for a million dollars," he became alarmed and asked, "How can I get them?" She answered, "Just ask for them, Colonel." A surprised and thankful Roosevelt soon had free supplies.

By the end of the war, Red Cross personnel had served in Cuba and the Philippines at the United States government's request. Finally in 1900—after the Spanish-American War had ended—the United States Congress formally granted a charter to the American Red Cross. The charter established the organization as

Hospital ships staffed by Red Cross nurses and medical corpsmen served as floating infirmaries during the war.

the nation's *official* relief agency for civilians and military personnel and made it a semigovernmental organization accountable to—although not funded by—Congress.

A Change in Leadership

While Barton was helping the wounded in Cuba, the Red Cross auxiliaries at home continued to work without her direction. Soon the American public criticized Barton for her lack of administrative control over Red Cross offices. Some volunteer leaders decided that she had to be removed from her leadership position.

Mabel Boardman, a Red Cross volunteer from a wealthy Ohio family, used her social connections to undermine Barton's control of the agency. She built a case for Barton's removal through a

Socialite Mabel Boardman forced Barton's resignation and took over the leadership of the Red Cross.

series of incidents that involved the Congress and even President Theodore Roosevelt. Many supporters urged Barton to fight the accusations that she was a poor administrator. But at age 82, she was feeling old and tired and didn't want the Red Cross to suffer from any of the bad publicity that such a conflict would attract. So in 1904, she reluctantly resigned from the organization that she had founded. She died at age 90 on April 12, 1912, in her Glen Echo, Maryland home.

Many of Barton's supporters left the organization after she stepped down. But Boardman and her assistants continued to run the Red Cross from a room in the army and navy building in Washington, D.C. Some wondered if the agency would still operate effectively during emergencies. Boardman, who used her own money to run the Red Cross, also had misgivings. But eventually, she led the organization into a new era of service.

Boardman approached Red Cross work differently than her predecessor had. Barton, despite her basic shyness, had been active in relief operations, delegated little work, and even had herself appointed "president for life." Although she was demanding of her staff, she expected even more of herself and was dedicated to helping people.

Unlike Barton, Boardman was more comfortable directing operations from her office and forming committees to make major decisions. During disasters, she turned over the responsibility for carrying out Red Cross work to specialists and saved her energies for directing the organization's work. Boardman refused to be a paid president and remained a volunteer throughout her life.

When Barton had run the Red Cross, some had criticized the agency's inability to coordinate the work of its branches. Boardman and her central committee (which made the organization's major decisions) resolved this problem. The committee abolished the independent Red Cross associations and replaced them with local chapters, the first step toward nationwide unity among Red Cross branches.

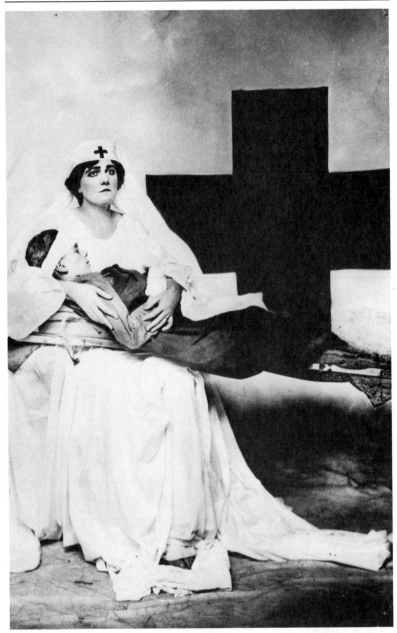

This photograph served as the basis for a poster that reflected the Red Cross's growth and public image.

FOUR

Growth
and Development

In 1905, Congress granted the American Red Cross the revised charter that it still follows. Like the original charter of 1900, the revised one permitted the agency to provide assistance when disasters struck, to care for the sick and wounded in the armed forces, and to help the government carry out the terms of the Geneva Conventions. But the revised charter also required the formation of a central committee with direct governmental representation. It allowed the president of the United States to appoint the committee chairperson as well as five committee members from the Justice, Navy, State, Treasury, and War Departments. It also required the Red Cross to provide Congress with an annual report for accounting purposes and made it a federal crime for any person or company to use the Red Cross emblem without the agency's permission. These provisions gave the organization its true semigovernmental status.

Within a year, the nation called on the Red Cross to perform its chartered relief services during one of the worst disasters in the nation's history—the San Francisco earthquake. At 5:12 A.M. on April 18, 1906, a devastating earthquake brought buildings crashing down in San Francisco, California. Fire swept the city, destroying miles of houses and buildings. Thousands of shocked and homeless victims, in desperate need of food and shelter, wandered the streets where troops patrolled to prevent looting.

At the time of the earthquake, all of the Red Cross workers who had experience in disaster relief had retired or resigned, and the agency's financial reserves were extremely low. Nevertheless, President Theodore Roosevelt ordered the Red Cross into action. To help the agency in its relief efforts, Roosevelt asked the American people to send contributions to the Red Cross because it was "the only organization chartered and authorized by Congress to act at times of great national calamity." This call to duty gave the American Red Cross the national recognition it

Despite staff shortages and a lack of funds, the Red Cross sheltered and fed victims of the 1906 earthquake in San Francisco.

needed to work effectively in this disaster.

The Red Cross quickly acquired the necessary skills to become a national relief organization capable of handling any emergency. It developed procedures in casework (social work and information collection for individuals who need assistance) that it continued to use for decades. It led and coordinated relief efforts with other organizations. And soon the Red Cross regained the respect of Americans who had watched the Barton-Boardman power struggle and had wondered if the organization would ever match its past glory.

After the San Francisco earthquake, the Red Cross donated money to victims based on their needs and provided all assistance for free. This disaster relief policy, which it still follows today, helped make victims self-sufficient without plunging them into debt through loans.

In the year of the San Francisco disaster, the American Red Cross also provided relief abroad. It sent money to Japan to help famine victims, to Italy for victims of the Mount Vesuvius volcanic eruption, and to Chile for earthquake victims. Generous Americans donated money to help those in need whenever disaster struck—abroad or at home.

And at home in America, the Red Cross broadened its scope to aid those affected by mining and other industrial accidents. The organization mounted a public education campaign to draw attention to the lives wasted in these mishaps. "Statistics show," Boardman wrote, "that in our mines alone over seven men are killed a day and nearly twenty injured." The problem attracted even greater publicity when a mine shaft collapsed at Cherry, Illinois, in 1909, killing more than 250 miners. To aid the miners' widows and children, the Red Cross set up a pension fund for them. The agency also convinced legislators that companies needed to take better care of their employees. As a result, Congress enacted the Workmen's Compensation laws that are still in effect today.

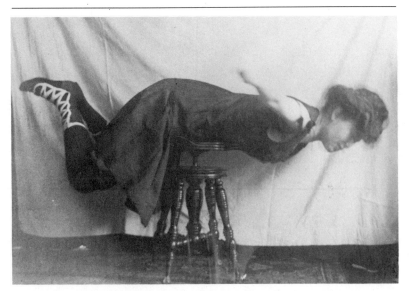

For years before the Red Cross offered swimming instruction, students practiced their swim strokes on land.

In addition to disaster relief, the Red Cross began to offer other services to the American public in the early 1900s. For example, the organization introduced Americans to water-safety education designed to protect nonswimmers from drowning. The need for this service became shockingly apparent when the excursion boat *Eastland* capsized, killing 812 people in waters near a Chicago dock in 1915.

The pioneer of Red Cross water safety was Commodore Wilbert E. Longfellow, a large man affectionately known as the "amiable whale." As the head of the Red Cross Life Saving Corps, Longfellow established "water first aid" as a Red Cross service in 1914. Before Longfellow's time, swimming instructors focused on "land drills," draping their beginning students over piano stools to practice swimming strokes in mid-air. Unlike these instructors, Longfellow believed that a person had to be in the water to learn good swimming skills. For 40 years, Longfellow taught Red Cross water safety in canals, at beaches, and wherever he could gather

Commodore Longfellow took swimmers out of the classroom and into the water. The "amiable whale" taught for 40 years.

students. His work eventually led to the development of the Life Saving Corps and evolved into a popular array of courses that still include such things as lifeguard training, emergency first aid, swimming lessons for the handicapped, and safety instruction for those who operate small boats.

Red Cross War Efforts

The large-scale battlefield relief envisioned by Dunant became a reality when the American Red Cross sent doctors and nurses overseas in 1914 at the outbreak of World War I. These medical teams arrived in Germany, Austria, Hungary, and other European nations to help the sick and wounded. At first, the agency followed its policy of neutrality, helping all of the wounded on both sides of the battle line.

In 1916, however, the British forced the Red Cross to change this policy. Fearing that the Germans might recycle the rubber in surgical gloves and other items to make tires and other war supplies, the British stopped Red Cross shipments of these goods into the German zone. Without these supplies, Red Cross workers found it difficult to function effectively in hospitals.

At the same time, Red Cross funds dipped dramatically. Because the United States was not involved in the fighting, Americans quickly lost interest in the war and contributed less money for medical relief. The Red Cross had to withdraw nearly all of its workers because of this lack of funds and the British supply embargo. However, it continued to offer some battlefield relief until the next year.

On April 6, 1917, the United States declared war against Germany. This declaration quickly ended the American Red Cross's policy of neutrality—and its financial problems. Reflecting the patriotism of the day, the agency decided to serve only soldiers of the United States and Allied nations. However, it pledged to give medical assistance to all prisoners of war. The same surge of patriotism moved Americans to donate their time and money to

Red Cross nurses sheltered orphans in sandbagged bunkers while the Germans bombed Belgium in World War I.

Red Cross canteens boosted the morale of Allied troops.

the Red Cross to help in the war effort. The agency's small treasury soon filled with contributions. Millions of dollars surged in to finance war-relief programs for the next several years.

Jazz singer Al Jolson and other celebrities helped raise money for the Red Cross by performing at public benefits and donating their time. President Woodrow Wilson also gave a boost to the agency's war efforts. He wanted the Red Cross to act as a "national shock absorber" during wartime, and believed that it was the natural organization to convert America's concern and volunteer spirit into effective wartime action. So he appointed a Red Cross War Council to make the major decisions affecting the organization and to raise millions of dollars to fund its activities. The War Council focused on Red Cross involvement in the war while Boardman and her central committee handled the routine business.

The organization accomplished incredible work overseas—especially in France, where Red Cross doctors and nurses staffed base hospitals. But it didn't work alone. Red Cross societies from other nations also offered battlefield relief. Red Cross workers also staffed recreation huts and canteens to keep up the morale of the Allied troops and launched a massive effort to help civilian refugees.

45

On the battlefields of Europe, Red Cross workers did not sit behind the lines and wait for work to come to them. For instance, the Outpost Service advanced with the troops and provided hot beverages and food. In one battle alone, Red Cross workers served 160,000 gallons of hot cocoa. Ambulance sections, consisting of more than 4,000 drivers and other staff members, rescued the wounded while under fire. Many Red Cross workers were decorated for bravery and some died, including 269 nurses who served on and off the battlefield.

Posters and popular songs, such as "The Rose of No-Man's Land," depicted the Red Cross nurse as a heroine. Even prisoners of war felt strongly about the nurses. Many of them showed their sorrow and appreciation when Jane Delano died, in 1919. Delano, a former superintendent of the Army Nurse Corps, joined the Red Cross in 1912 and reorganized the agency's nurse corps. She was dedicated to nursing the Allied troops as well as their prisoners. After she died in a field hospital in France, German prisoners of war stood up as her coffin passed and saluted—a show of gratitude for all of the help that American Red Cross nurses had given them.

Delano reorganized the agency's nursing corps and became a heroine to many soldiers.

The agency taught these firemen to knit for the war effort.

At home in America, volunteers flocked to local Red Cross chapters to help in any way they could. For the American troops in the trenches of Europe, they made bandages, packed prisoner-of-war relief boxes, and even knitted mittens and socks. Local chapters turned out 343 million items, including hospital supplies and dressings, personal articles for servicemen, and clothing for refugees.

They also offered services to the troops at home. Throughout the country, volunteers served refreshments to soldiers at train stations, handed out donated items in hospitals, and wrote letters for the wounded. Volunteers of all ages felt it was their patriotic duty to support the organization. By the time Red Cross war services ended in February 1919, the organization boasted 31 million volunteers. On the home front, these volunteers combatted an epidemic of Spanish influenza that killed more than 500,000 Americans in 1918. Red Cross nurses risked their own lives to aid sick civilians and soldiers.

The Junior Red Cross volunteer program, now a part of Community Services, began in America during World War I. The pro-

Millions of youngsters joined local chapters of the Junior Red Cross to help children in war-torn nations.

gram was the idea of Vassar College President Dr. Henry Noble McCracken, who wanted to give America's youth the chance to help children in foreign lands. President Wilson endorsed McCracken's idea and established the first Junior Red Cross in September of 1917, advising youngsters to share in the "cause of freedom." These young volunteers' duties included making splints, specially-prepared foods, surgical dressings, and even furniture for hospitals and convalescent homes. By the end of World War I, 11 million young people swelled the ranks of the Junior Red Cross.

The armistice ending the war was signed on November 11, 1918, but the Red Cross did not leave Europe. European refugees still needed help in the countries where fighting had raged—and the need seemed endless. The last of the American Red Cross personnel withdrew from Europe in 1922.

Peacetime Programs

In 1919, Henry P. Davison, an American banker and the chairman of the Red Cross War Council, proposed that national Red Cross societies band together to end world suffering through united action. He believed that all of the societies should share the heavy strain of service to mankind. President Wilson, who was in Paris for a peace conference, wholeheartedly endorsed Davison's idea. The council then presented the proposal to representatives from Great Britain, Italy, France, and Japan. It assured them that the new organization would not undermine the role of the International Committee of the Red Cross, the all-Swiss group dedicated to the promotion of the Geneva Conventions. The meeting in Paris led to the establishment of the League of Red Cross and Red Crescent Societies. Today, 137 international Red Cross societies make up that league.

The American Red Cross shifted from wartime to peacetime services following World War I. At the height of the war, the agency had had more than 20 million adult members and 3,864 chapters providing community services and assisting military personnel and refugees overseas. When the motivation of the war effort ended, however, contributions plummeted and volunteers left—forcing the chapters and the national headquarters to cut staff and trim budgets.

In order to continue to provide humanitarian services at home and abroad, the Red Cross wanted to avoid becoming a small organization again. However, most people were reluctant to volunteer their services in peacetime, and the agency was in danger of shrinking.

In 1919, after months of studying the situation, Red Cross leaders presented the American public with a new peacetime program. The agency wanted to prepare the public to deal with disasters, establish a public health program, provide first aid instruction, and expand Junior Red Cross activities. Agency leaders also decided to spend less money on overseas activities so they could concentrate on community health activities at home.

The peacetime program called for one million more volunteers. Although chapter members canvassed door-to-door to try to attract new members, the decline in volunteers and donations continued. By the end of the campaign, the Red Cross had only 8 million volunteers—down from more than 20 million in 1918. Despite its admirable intentions, the proposed peacetime program had failed to motivate the public.

The failure of the 1919 campaign forced the Red Cross to rethink its role in the lives of American citizens. So in 1921, the organization began to look closely at what the public wanted— instead of what its leaders thought the public wanted. The agency found that, although public health services in community centers had slipped in popularity, other programs (which are still part of the Red Cross today) had gained support. The Junior Red Cross

Public demand expanded the agency's water-safety program.

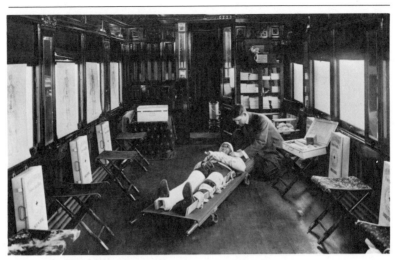

First aid trains functioned as traveling classrooms.

remained popular, as did services for veterans and military personnel. Disaster relief continued to be a vital service, and the public wanted more first aid and water-safety instruction—a demand that kept Red Cross instructors busy.

To meet this demand, the Red Cross used first aid trains. In this innovative training program, the agency taught first aid classes in specially designed Pullman cars. The cars were equipped as a lecture room, a kitchen, an office, and sleeping quarters for the staff. The trains stopped all over the country at railway yards, where staff members taught railroad workers and others how to handle on-the-job injuries. Eventually, the Red Cross moved from teaching first aid skills in trains to providing instruction in schools, factories, and military bases.

The Depression Years

America faced a number of national tragedies in the 1930s, and the Red Cross was there to help. Although natural disasters struck with frequency, a man-made catastrophe—the stock market crash

Red Cross seed packages helped drought-stricken farmers replant their fields.

of 1929—posed the greatest challenge for the country and the Red Cross. The Depression following the stock market crash drained many families of their entire savings. As coal mines and factories closed and businesses failed, throwing employees by the thousands out into the streets, breadlines became common in the nation's cities.

Although the Red Cross faced this heavy challenge at a time when its own donations were shrinking, ironically, the Depression years also helped the organization by spurring a renewed interest in volunteer work. Volunteer ranks grew as Americans committed themselves to helping each other. Between 1929 and 1933, the Red Cross funneled millions of dollars of aid to the victims of the Depression.

During the same period, widespread drought scorched the midwestern plains and turned once lush fields into dusty lands overrun by hungry grasshoppers. Rural families in these areas—dependent on crops for their livelihoods—needed food and clothing. Many sold everything they had just to survive. In 1930, President Herbert Hoover called on the Red Cross to aid drought victims. The agency tried to help on its own, providing assistance through money from public contributions.

More than 37,000 Red Cross volunteers collected clothing and food for distribution throughout the drought-stricken areas. Workers interviewed drought victims and gave them purchase orders to present to storekeepers for flour, milk, meat, clothing, and other necessities. At the end of the month, storekeepers sent the bills for these items to local Red Cross chapters for payment. Chapters that didn't have enough money to pay these bills asked the national Red Cross headquarters for funds. And the bills poured in.

Critics of the relief operation argued that Congress should provide money for the Red Cross so that the agency could serve more people, including all of America's unemployed. The Red Cross had always refused federal aid in order to avoid government interference, and it wasn't willing to change this policy. Its leaders argued that the agency could always rely on the public for financial

The agency obtained government food for the unemployed.

aid during a crisis. Newspapers supported the Red Cross stand and hailed the organization as a symbol of American self-reliance. But helping drought victims and the nation's unemployed soon became more than the agency could handle alone.

Finally, Red Cross leaders saw the wisdom of accepting federal aid so that the organization could help more people. In 1933, the agency and the federal government combined forces to combat the Depression and the drought that had devastated America. Accepting federal aid, the Red Cross distributed the government's surplus of wheat, grain, and other products to the hungry throughout the country. More than six million families received assistance through programs sponsored by the agency and the federal government. Eventually, the federal government assumed many Red Cross volunteer services.

In the 1930s, the Red Cross accepted new duties and began to work closely with other agencies under President Franklin D. Roosevelt's New Deal legislation, which promoted economic recovery and social reform. For example, it gave on-the-job first aid instruction to more than 48,000 workers at the request of the

President Roosevelt (right) supported the Red Cross, which presented him with a membership pin in 1934.

54

Civilian Conservation Corps workers loaded food onto Red Cross trucks for delivery to midwestern flood victims.

Civil Works Administration. It also combined its efforts with those of the Civilian Conservation Corps, which helped deliver Red Cross food packages to flood victims in the Midwest. The Red Cross helped sustain the nation while its economy recovered in the late 1930s and the early 1940s.

The Red Cross and World War II

For nearly two years before America entered World War II, the Red Cross assisted European war victims from countries occupied by Nazi Germany. It shipped ambulances to England and Finland and packed tons of flour, milk products, medical supplies, and other lifesaving items for shipment to other European countries.

On December 7, 1941, when the Japanese bombed the United States Naval base at Pearl Harbor, Hawaii, America entered World

War II. The government turned its attention to military matters abroad, and the American Red Cross resumed its position as a full-fledged wartime relief agency. At home, it mobilized civilians into volunteer action, setting the stage for one of the agency's most important achievements—the blood donor program.

The Red Cross had drawn its first unit of blood at the Augusta, Georgia, chapter in 1937, and had opened a voluntary blood-donor service at a New York City hospital before the war. As the war progressed, the government began to rely on the agency for blood and plasma (the fluid part of blood) to prevent shock and save lives on battlefields. In earlier wars, shock (usually from blood loss) had killed more soldiers than the wounds themselves. In World War II, the use of plasma reversed this trend. By the end of the war, the American Red Cross had drawn more than 13

During the war, army medics saved countless lives with blood and plasma collected in Red Cross donation drives.

This Disney cartoon helped boost Red Cross membership.

million pints of blood for military use, saving countless lives. In fact, the blood plasma it obtained during the war would have filled New York's Empire State Building.

The resurgence of patriotism during World War II resulted in increased volunteerism for the American Red Cross, and the agency grew to its largest size since World War I. As they had done in the first world war, volunteers flocked to help the war effort. During the peak period between 1939 (when the war began in Europe) and 1946 (when the troops began to come back), more than seven million Red Cross volunteers labored at home. The Junior Red Cross rapidly expanded to 20 million members, who helped adult volunteers with a variety of projects, including the making of stretchers for the wounded and splints for broken bones. And more than 36 million individuals contributed money.

In Red Cross warehouses across the country, volunteers packaged weekly supplies for more than 1 million Allied and 115,000 American prisoners of war. These supply packages saved many prisoners of war from starvation. If all of these packages had been

The agency sent millions of packages from its warehouses.

placed end to end, they would have stretched from Chicago, Illinois, to Berlin, Germany.

During the war, providing services to the Allied Forces all over the world cost the Red Cross more than $365 million. And at home, 4 million volunteers joined the more than 141 million overseas volunteers who worked with the American military in emergency and recreation services. As always, the Red Cross could count on its volunteers.

When the war ended in 1945, the Red Cross turned its attention to the millions of war refugees all over the world. The agency assisted relief teams from the newly-formed United Nations in feeding, sheltering, transporting, and reuniting families displaced by the war.

The Postwar Years

Hoping to avoid a decline in support and, therefore, preparedness, such as the one that had followed World War I, Red Cross leaders decided to modernize the agency for peacetime. They knew that they would receive fewer contributions and that Red Cross volunteers would return to their prewar occupations when the war ended.

At the National Convention of the Red Cross in 1947, the leaders announced major changes in the organization's structure and functions. For example, they created a board of governors consisting of presidential appointees, members elected by the board itself, and representatives from local chapters. This mix of board members made the agency responsive to national *and* local concerns. The leaders also established a peacetime blood program to meet the day-to-day transfusion needs of American civilians.

But after World War II, America's peacetime was short-lived. On June 25, 1950, North Korean Communists invaded South Korea. Through an undeclared war called a police action, the United States

Clothing donated by the Red Cross aided Korean children orphaned by war.

led the United Nations coalition that stepped in to help South Korea. And once again, the Red Cross became a vital part of the American war effort.

As authorized by its congressional charter, the American Red Cross provided a variety of services to keep up the morale of the Americans serving their country overseas. An executive order by President Harry Truman named the Red Cross the nation's official source of whole blood and plasma for the wounded. In all of these activities, the Red Cross did not limit its support to the American soldiers but assisted all United Nations forces in Korea.

During the Korean conflict, the military's use of helicopters to speed injured soldiers to the nearest field hospitals for treatment cut the death toll dramatically. And Red Cross plasma and other blood products kept the wounded from going into shock before they reached the hospitals. In fact, because of the widespread use of plasma, there were 50 percent fewer deaths due to shock than there had been in World War II.

Helicopters allowed medics in Korea to administer Red Cross plasma to the wounded before they reached field hospitals.

After the 1956 Hungarian revolt, Red Cross workers signaled Hungarian refugees attempting to cross the Austrian border.

When the Korean conflict ended in 1953, the Red Cross worked closely with the United Nations to coordinate the exchange of 87,000 prisoners of war between the United Nations forces and the Communists. This operation—known as "Big Switch"—involving both American and Korean Red Cross societies, was the first in a series of relief services to postwar victims.

In the years after the Korean conflict, the American Red Cross continued to provide disaster relief at home. It also organized several major relief operations for refugees fleeing totalitarian regimes and poor living conditions. For example, when the Hungarians revolted against Communist rule in the fall of 1956, the League of Red Cross Societies appealed to the American Red Cross for help. Thousands of Hungarian freedom fighters, whose only weapons were rocks and gasoline bombs, died while fighting Soviet tanks. Tens of thousands more, however, escaped on foot

61

Hungarians were reunited at Red Cross refugee centers.

from war-torn Hungary—most carrying nothing more than a suitcase. To assist these refugees, the International Red Cross set up centers in neighboring Austria. The refugee centers—four of which were run by the American Red Cross—provided many services, including resettlement for the homeless. Eventually, more than 200,000 Hungarians fled from their country. Many of them found help at the American Red Cross centers. Back in the United States, the Red Cross packaged and sent supplies to riot victims in Hungary and set up refugee centers in New York City and at Camp Kilmer, New Jersey. Refugee work continued in these centers until 1957.

In 1961, the United States government asked the American Red Cross to coordinate a major relief operation after the failed Bay of Pigs invasion, during which United States-backed Cuban exiles had attacked the Communist island of Cuba and been captured. Cuban president Fidel Castro agreed to release the prisoners and their relatives living in Cuba in exchange for food and medical supplies amounting to more than $53 million. The American Red Cross worked with the Cuban Red Cross to help make this exchange possible. By the summer of 1963, more than 9,000 Cubans had sailed to freedom aboard Red Cross chartered ships.

The American Red Cross and its workers had saved the lives of more than 1,000 Cubans. The United States Postal Service honored the organization by issuing a commemorative stamp depicting a Red Cross flag flying from a rescue ship. In 1980, the Red Cross again assisted Cuban refugees at the government's request when more than 116,000 Cubans and Haitians fled their homelands for America.

In 1964, Congress passed legislation that allowed the Red Cross to use its funds more efficiently for disaster relief, refugee work, and other services. The legislation—passed after the Good Friday earthquake in Anchorage, Alaska—directed the govern-

The agency rushed in when an earthquake rocked Anchorage.

ment to make funds available to homeowners who owed money on their mortgages. It allowed the Red Cross to get out of the costly business of home rehabilitation and to concentrate on the emergency phase of disaster operations and other forms of relief work.

During the Vietnam War from 1964 to 1973, the Red Cross sent workers to Vietnam to help servicepeople with personal and emergency needs at hospitals and bases. When the North Vietnamese refused to treat American prisoners of war according to

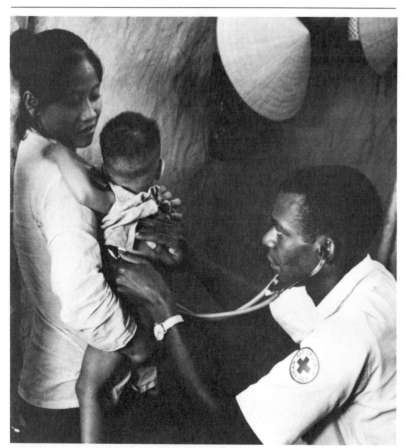

During the Vietnam War, Red Cross medical personnel provided health care to Vietnamese refugees.

the Geneva Conventions, the agency cosponsored a resolution with the United States government that asked all nations to renew their pledge to the Geneva Convention's principles. The resolution was adopted unanimously.

At the end of the Vietnam War, the Red Cross faced one of the world's worst refugee problems. When the South Vietnamese government collapsed, the agency organized Operation New Life to help tens of thousands of Indo-Chinese fleeing Communist rule. The operation established refugee camps throughout the Pacific, so that workers and other volunteers could process the paperwork and resettle the homeless Indo-Chinese. Throughout the United States, thousands of Red Cross volunteers and staff members assisted the refugees with transportation, English lessons, and other services needed to adjust to life in America. Thanks to the efforts of the American Red Cross, more than 130,000 refugees found new homes in America.

HELP
RED
CROSS
HELP

. . . the UNITED WAY

The Red Cross finances most of its programs through donations. Posters such as the one above encourage giving.

FIVE

Inside the
Organization

The structure of the American Red Cross resembles a wagon wheel. The national headquarters in Washington, D.C., is the hub of the wheel, and the five operational, or regional, headquarters are the spokes. Three operational headquarters serve the United States: the Alexandria, Virginia, office covers the eastern third of the nation; the St. Louis, Missouri, headquarters handles the midwestern third; and the Burlingame, California, facility serves the western third. The Red Cross maintains two other operational offices in Germany and Japan to serve American military personnel and their families overseas. More than 2,900 chapters and 57 blood centers make up the wheel's outer rim. In this system, the chapters, operational headquarters, and national headquarters share resources.

The national headquarters provides the overall policy administration and guidance for the organization. About 2,000 employees form the national staff, and at least 200 of them work with military installations overseas.

The American Red Cross Organization

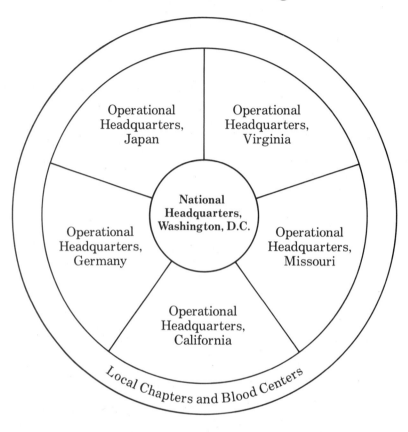

The three operational headquarters guide the local chapters in their area to maintain the consistency that a large organization with a multimillion-dollar budget needs to be successful. Key Resource Chapters (KRCs) help the operational headquarters handle this responsibility by assisting smaller chapters when possible. KRCs have enough money, people, and material to operate without help from the national and operational headquarters.

Each local chapter, which usually covers a territory about the size of a county, conducts the services required by the congressional charter. Chapters may also provide other programs that meet the particular needs of the community they serve. Chapters that frequently need support from the national sector or KRCs to carry out their chartered duties are part of Field Service Territories. This makes it easier for other offices to assist them regularly.

When a major disaster strikes, the national and operational headquarters determine what assistance the affected area needs and work closely with the local chapter to provide it. This gives the chapter a leadership role in its own community while making national resources available.

For example, if a flood occurs in West Virginia, the Eastern Operational Headquarters reviews the situation with the local chapter in the stricken community. If the chapter doesn't have enough resources to cope with the disaster by itself, the operational headquarters sends personnel from other areas for assistance and sup-

The agency supervises local chapters from its Washington, D.C., headquarters building, a national landmark.

plies additional money to give victims immediate relief. In a major disaster, every community can count on assistance geared to meet the victims' needs, even if the Red Cross must shift personnel from one coast to another to do so.

Coordinating Efforts

The American Red Cross works closely with several federal agencies. For instance, whenever a major disaster threatens a part of the country, the Red Cross coordinates its relief efforts with state and federal officials, especially those in the Federal Emergency Management Agency (FEMA).

Typically, the Red Cross and FEMA divide relief duties to ensure help for disaster victims. The Red Cross provides food, clothing, shelter, blood, and medical care to disaster victims. When the disaster is over, it helps families become self-sufficient again— including those who are not eligible for government assistance. Depending on the nature of the disaster, the Red Cross may also post warnings, help evacuate a city or town, supply trained volunteers to assist in rescue work, and transport household goods to storage areas.

FEMA and other government agencies protect the lives and property of disaster victims and provide public health, police, fire, and sanitation services. They also establish emergency communication and transportation services and set up temporary morgues. When the emergency has passed, these government agencies work to restore the area and help the victims obtain other forms of federal assistance. Finally, they offer business loans and issue food stamps and surplus foods to those who qualify.

When a crisis strikes, the Red Cross can also join forces with state and local governments. For example, in 1979 the organization mobilized more than 2,000 volunteers to help in the potential evacuation of Three Mile Island, Pennsylvania, the scene of a nuclear power plant accident. Fortunately, state and local officials

After a disaster, Red Cross volunteers may post notices informing victims of available aid.

confined the radiation contamination, making evacuation unnecessary.

In addition to FEMA, the American Red Cross works with other federal agencies to provide health care and safety services. For instance, it cooperates with the United States Department of Health and Human Services to promote the use of seat belts and the training of at least one person in every household to give cardiopulmonary resuscitation (CPR).

Because it provides so many services to military personnel, the Red Cross also work closely with the United States Department of Defense. Red Cross representatives who work in this capacity use offices supplied by the department and, in wartime, may travel with the military to combat zones.

To help its programs run more smoothly, the Red Cross works with other organizations, such as the American Legion and the Salvation Army, as well as various labor, church, and community groups.

Leading the Red Cross

More than 20,000 paid employees and 1,700,000 active adult volunteers (excluding blood donors) carry out the work of the American Red Cross. These staff members and volunteers receive guidance from Red Cross officials, including the board of governors, executive committee, president, and chapter boards of directors.

The board of governors, the governing body of the American Red Cross, consists of 50 volunteer members. The board's honorary chairperson, the president of the United States, appoints eight board members, including the official chairperson, who presides at board meetings. The board itself elects 12 members, and chapter representatives elect the remaining 30 members. The

In 1983, the board of governors selected Richard F. Schubert as the Red Cross's president.

board also selects the agency's president, a salaried employee, who is responsible for carrying out the organization's policies and programs.

A volunteer board of directors, made up of community members, guides each local Red Cross chapter according to the policies established by the board of governors. However, if a local board of directors wishes, its chapter can tailor national programs to meet the needs of its community.

Funding the Red Cross

The Red Cross relies on public donations to fund most of its community programs. Contributions to the general Red Cross fund account for about 33 percent of overall annual revenues and finance most ongoing services. Special fund-raising campaigns cover the costs of relief services for major domestic or overseas disasters.

Contributions generally come to the Red Cross through its local chapters. Many chapters receive some contributions directly from the public. Many others receive money from The United Way, a national fund-raising organization. The chapters then give some of this money to the national Red Cross headquarters. The national office uses part of the contributions to help defray the expenses of running a nationwide relief agency. It also uses part of them to aid military personnel stationed at American bases around the world. It saves the rest to give to the local chapters when chartered responsibilities push them beyond their means.

The Red Cross funds its blood program by using the cost-recovery principle: It meets the expenses of its 57 blood centers by charging the nation's hospitals processing fees for blood used. To help recover expenses for nursing, first aid, and health-training courses, the agency recently instituted modest fees. However, it never turns people in need away from a course because they lack money.

Rescuing flood victims is part of disaster relief, one of the many services offered by today's Red Cross.

SIX

Red Cross Programs Today

Traditionally, the American Red Cross has concentrated on providing two major services—battlefield relief and disaster relief. In fact, the government acknowledges the Red Cross as the best-equipped agency to feed, shelter, and handle casework for victims of major disasters. Today's Red Cross also provides a wide range of services, such as nutritional education, health professional training, famine relief, blood collection, and many others.

Health and Safety Programs

In 1981, a Red Cross study revealed a relationship between good health habits and longevity. It also showed that healthier American lifestyles could reduce the cost of medical bills. The study's findings prompted the Red Cross to develop major health programs designed to help Americans avoid stress, improve nutrition, and increase exercise.

As a result, local chapters of the Red Cross now offer a variety of health and safety programs throughout the United States. For example, the agency provides free blood pressure checks in black communities, where hypertension (abnormally high blood pressure) poses a serious health problem. Chapters also offer nutrition programs, exercise groups, and other health-related activities.

Standard health and safety courses, such as swimming instruction, remain popular. But the Red Cross offers other courses, too, including kayaking and sailing instruction, aquatics for the disabled, high blood pressure awareness, multiple sclerosis home care, safe baby-sitting, and parenthood preparation. It awards certificates of achievement to more than six million people each year for participation in health and safety courses.

Local chapters rely on trained volunteers to teach all of the courses. (Instructor training courses are available to volunteers who have completed general courses.) Special programs teach volunteers and health professionals how to function when faced with life-threatening disasters. The Red Cross also trains personnel for safety-related jobs, such as lifeguarding at swimming pools and other recreational sites.

The Adapted Aquatics program teaches handicapped people water safety techniques.

*The Red Cross
teaches artificial
respiration, which
helped this fireman
save a baby.*

First Aid Instruction

Since 1906 the Red Cross has offered first aid instruction in American communities on a regular basis. Today, the agency is the acknowledged expert in this field. One of the most important first aid skills it teaches is artificial respiration, which is often used in drowning incidents. To perform this lifesaving technique, the rescuer gives the victim the "kiss of life"—a procedure requiring the rescuer to blow air into the victim's mouth. This procedure is designed to trigger the victim's lungs to operate on their own, getting the breathing process started again. If artificial respiration doesn't work, the rescuer may try CPR.

The American Red Cross also teaches CPR—a lifesaving skill developed by the American Heart Association. In this technique, the rescuer forces air into the victim's mouth and applies pressure to his chest. The purpose is to start the heart and lungs operating on their own. This method is useful for drowning and heart-attack victims. Since 1974, when the Red Cross began teaching this form of first aid, it has taught millions of Americans to perform CPR.

Red Cross workers can use telecommunications equipment to transmit urgent information for soldiers overseas.

Services to the Armed Forces

The American Red Cross offers personal services—including emergency help 24 hours a day—to military personnel at home and abroad. For example, a soldier serving in a foreign country may be needed at home because a close relative is critically ill. The Red Cross chapter in the hometown can contact the relative's doctor to verify the urgency of the situation. The chapter will then transmit the information to the Red Cross national headquarters in Washington, D.C. In turn, the headquarters will send the information over high-speed teletype machines to the military base in the foreign country. The Red Cross worker at the base who receives this information will then contact the soldier and his commanding officer. After the commanding officer grants emergency leave, the Red Cross will even help arrange the soldier's travel plans and provide travel money, if necessary.

The Red Cross also provides other types of assistance to members of the military. For instance, it helps spouses who fail to receive allotment checks because of pay problems. It also helps military personnel contact family members they have not heard from in a long time. Red Cross caseworkers assist service personnel with problems they may be facing on the base and help veterans obtain their Veterans Administration benefits.

Organ and Tissue Donations

In recent years, the growing demand for donor tissues and organs has moved the Red Cross to take on new responsibilities in this area of public health. The organization believes that organ, tissue, and bone marrow donations should be available to all who need them, regardless of the recipient's social or financial status or other considerations.

On July 31, 1986, the American Red Cross launched the nation's first central bone marrow registry. This program serves thousands of leukemia patients and others with blood diseases who need bone marrow transplants and can't find eligible donors. The registry, located in St. Paul, Minnesota, matches these patients with bone marrow donors.

At least 35 chapters retrieve donor bones from hospitals as part of a pilot program, and 2 chapters operate organ procurement centers. More than 200 Red Cross doctors and scientists work closely with hospitals and universities to study ways to preserve tissue and organs for transplantation.

Blood Collection

Across the nation, 57 regional blood centers collect, process, and distribute blood and blood products, such as plasma and blood platelets (the part of blood that stops bleeding). Every year, the blood centers collect more than six million units of blood. Blood

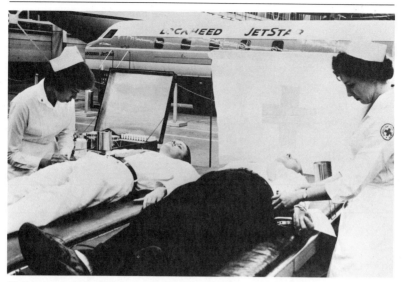

Volunteers take blood at workplaces during donor drives.

and blood products save the lives of many accident and burn victims and hemophiliacs (people who bleed uncontrollably after even a minor injury).

The Red Cross relies on donors—it does not pay people to give blood. Because paid blood donors might give blood even when they know they are seriously ill, this volunteer system promotes a safer blood supply. And because the Red Cross collects nearly half of the blood donated each year in America, this is an important consideration. Most people between age 17 and 66 can donate the "gift of life" at a Red Cross blood center. Those with rare blood types are especially in demand. Individuals can also donate during special blood collection drives, usually held in community centers, schools, and workplaces. The Red Cross encourages regular donations to avoid shortages in the blood supply when a major emergency, such as an airplane crash, occurs.

The agency also conducts blood research to improve immunity to serious diseases and to find new ways to preserve blood and blood products for longer periods of time.

AIDS Research

AIDS poses one of the greatest challenges to the Red Cross. Individuals can contract this life-threatening disease through sexual contact with others who have been exposed to it, drug abuse involving tainted needles, and infected blood transfusions. Because the Red Cross collects so much blood, it must work hard to keep this blood safe for transfusions. (Red Cross donors are in no danger of getting AIDS by giving blood; the agency destroys disposable, sterilized needles used for blood collection after one use.)

To help safeguard the nation's blood supply, the Red Cross submits every new blood donation to a laboratory screening test for the AIDS antibody and for the hepatitis virus. If the blood

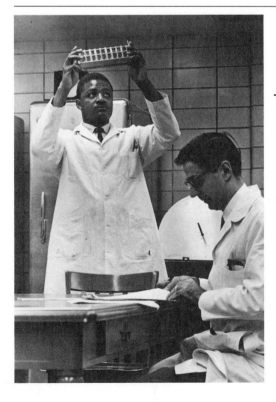

Technicians examine blood to determine blood type and to screen for the AIDS antibody.

contains AIDS virus antibodies or the hepatitis virus, Red Cross workers destroy the blood and notify the donor. However, the presence of AIDS antibodies only means that the individual has been exposed to the AIDS virus, not necessarily that he has the disease.

The Red Cross works closely with the federal government and other organizations in trying to stop the spread of AIDS. Since 1985, the agency has been educating people about the symptoms of AIDS and telling them how to avoid this fatal disease. In 1986, it launched a major educational campaign on AIDS through its many chapters, some of which set up "hot lines" for the public. It took on this large task because it recognized that the country had always counted on it when epidemics struck, such as the 1918 influenza epidemic.

America's Youth and the Red Cross

The Red Cross recognizes that America's young people need self-reliance and confidence to become future leaders of the country and of the organization. Therefore, it designs courses to build leadership skills through supervised volunteer tasks. Some courses try to help students understand themselves as well as others, and many courses develop organizational skills that can be used for recreation and everyday living. Red Cross courses aimed at America's youth include Basic First Aid, Alcohol Information, Good Grooming, Babysitting, and Facts for Life (life-management skills). Youths also perform adult duties within chapter programs, particularly those in safety and disaster fields.

Relief at Home and Abroad

Because millions of people in Third World nations die of starvation and disease each year, the American Red Cross has increased its role in helping these countries feed and care for their people.

A volunteer (right) consoles a Mexican woman who has lost a loved one in a disaster.

American contributions have supported major feeding, sheltering, and medical operations conducted by the International Red Cross, saving millions in such places as drought-stricken Africa and Thailand's border camps, where starving refugees flee from war-torn Cambodia.

Help for America's own impoverished poses another challenge for the Red Cross. For example, poor economic conditions in parts of the country, combined with laws that release certain mental patients from hospitals and other institutions, have created a new class of Americans who need help. Street people, found across the country, sleep wherever they can find shelter and eat whatever they can scavenge. More than 400 Red Cross chapters have received funds from the Emergency Food and Shelter National Board to provide services to America's homeless and hungry. Emergency legislation signed into law by President Ronald Reagan in November 1985 allocated millions of dollars to the national board, which Congress created in 1983 to deal with the estimated 300,000 to 2,000,000 homeless Americans. In addition to the chapters receiving money from the national board, another 75 Red Cross chapters help the homeless through other sources of funding, including public donations.

83

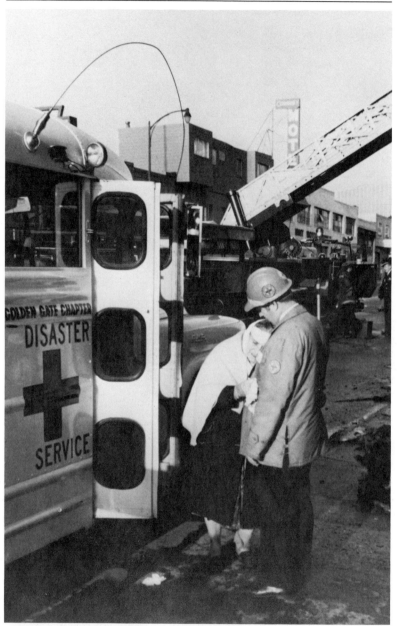

Red Cross volunteers will continue to offer physical and emotional comfort to victims of fires and other disasters.

SEVEN

Looking to the Future

In 1904, Clara Barton commented on the role of the Red Cross in American life: "It is not in its past that the glories or benefits of the Red Cross lie, but in the possibilities it has created for the future." Her statement is as true now as it was then. Today, the American Red Cross continues its commitment to the well-being of all the peoples of the world and is prepared to extend this pledge into the future.

The Red Cross symbol continues to shine as a beacon of hope throughout the world. In every emergency situation—in peacetime or in wartime—the Red Cross is there. The agency provides relief for victims of floods, earthquakes, hurricanes, and bombings. The Red Cross is the only agency that reaches out to help many homeless refugees. It boosts the morale of America's armed forces. And Red Cross workers are always ready to help those whose lives have been threatened by a war. Politics, race, and social status mean nothing to the organization. Human need is the only voice it hears.

Looking to the future, the Red Cross hopes to focus more of its energies and resources on emergency services at home and abroad and on improvements to its transplantation services and safety education programs. Helping Americans prepare for disasters and helping the victims of those disasters will be chief concerns. Finding ways to maintain disaster funds will continue to present problems because of the growing cost of providing relief. In places affected by starvation and drought, such as Africa, the American Red Cross will need to provide mass feedings and projects to save the land and crops for years to come. At home, the agency will have to care for a growing number of homeless and unemployed Americans. It will also need to educate citizens about AIDS prevention and continue research until a cure is found. Despite a long-standing, successful blood program, the agency will have to find new blood donors and keep the regular ones coming back if America's blood supply is to stay strong. Attracting volunteers to carry out the organization's work will also present a challenge.

The Red Cross fed starving African children in 1984. Feeding the hungry continues to be a challenge for the agency.

The agency's success in meeting these challenges depends on its ability to adapt. Although it is a nonprofit organization, the Red Cross has already recognized the need to become more businesslike in order to function efficiently. But it will still need increased financial support from all sources if it is to respond effectively to the public's needs. The Red Cross will need society's help.

As a volunteer organization, the Red Cross depends on people of all ages to help make the world a better place. Volunteers are still—more than 100 years since the agency's inception—its true strength. Their time and money make the Red Cross work— in natural disasters, in community programs, and on the battlefield. For them, the wisdom of the agency's humanitarian mission shines clearly:

> The mission of the American Red Cross is to improve the quality of human life; to enhance self-reliance and concern for others; and to help people avoid, prepare for, and cope with emergencies. It does this through services that are governed and directed by volunteers and are consistent with its congressional charter and the principles of the International Red Cross.

Fortunately, the American Red Cross has been able to rely on the support of its volunteers and the American public just as those who are in need can rely on the Red Cross.

GLOSSARY

AIDS - Acquired Immune Deficiency Syndrome, an immune disorder transmitted through the exchange of bodily fluids, such as blood.

Board of Directors - Community volunteers who make policy for their chapter and ensure that it adheres to the chartered responsibilities of the Red Cross.

Board of Governors - The 50-volunteer body that makes corporate policy for the American Red Cross.

Cardiopulmonary Resuscitation (CPR) - Lifesaving technique using both mouth-to-mouth breathing and chest pressure to revive a victim of heart attack, choking, or drowning.

Chapter - Local branch of the Red Cross.

Chartered - Authorized by the United States Congress to perform certain functions on behalf of the country.

Field office - Red Cross office on a military base.

Hemophiliac - Person with a hereditary blood disorder that prevents normal clotting and results in excessive bleeding after even a minor injury.

Outpost Service - World War I Red Cross service to troops fighting in the frontline trenches.

Plasma - The fluid part of blood. It helps prevent shock following a major injury.

Third World nation - Newly developed country struggling to become self-sufficient.

United Way - Organization that coordinates a single, annual fund-raising campaign for a number of charitable groups.

SELECTED REFERENCES

Barton, Clara. *A Story of the Red Cross*. New York: Airmont Publishing Company, 1968.

Dulles, Foster Rhea. *The American Red Cross: A History*. New York: Harper & Brothers Publishers, 1950.

Dunant, Henry. *A Memory of Solferino*. Washington, D.C.: The American Red Cross, 1959.

Fishwick, Marshall W. *Clara Barton*. Illustrious Americans. Morristown, N.J.: Silver Burdett Co., 1966.

Gilbo, Patrick F. *The American Red Cross: The First Century*. New York: Harper & Row, 1981.

Gilbo, Patrick F. "Candid, 'Cranky' Clara Barton Gave Us the Red Cross." *Smithsonian*, Volume 12, No. 2 (May 1981): 126–142.

Hurd, Charles. *The Compact History of the American Red Cross*. New York: Hawthorn Books, Inc., 1959.

Levathes, Louise. "The American Red Cross: A Century of Service." *National Geographic*, Volume 159, No. 6 (June 1981): 777–791.

Ross, Ishbel. *Angel of the Battlefield: The Life of Clara Barton*. New York: Harper & Brothers Publishers, 1956.

ACKNOWLEDGMENT

The author and publisher are grateful to the American Red Cross for information and photographs.

89

INDEX

A

administration 72, 73
affirmative action 12
AIDS research 81, 82, 86
  screening 82
Alexandria, Virginia 67
American Association of the Red
  Cross 29
American Heart Association 77
American Legion 71
American National Red Cross 33
Appia, Louis 25
armbands 24
armed forces programs 78, 79
Armenia 33
Army Nurse Corps 46
Arthur, Chester A. 29
artificial respiration 77
attorney general 8
Austria 21, 23

B

Baden 24
Barton, Clara 27–37, 41, 85
Battle of Solferino 21–23, 27
Bavaria 24
Bay of Pigs 62
Big Switch 61
blood collection 17, 56, 59, 79,
  80, 86
board of directors 73, 88
board of governors 59, 72, 73, 88
Boardman, Mabel 36, 37, 41, 45
bone marrow registry 79
Bryce, James 9
Burlingame, California 67
business 11, 13, 14

C

cabinet 9, 11
cardiopulmonary resuscitation
  (CPR) 71, 77, 88

Castro, Fidel 63
central committee 39, 45
Chile 41
civil rights 12
civil service 9, 10
Civil Service Commission 10
Civil War 9, 27
Civil Works Administration 55
Civilian Conservation Corps 55
Community Services 47
Congress 35, 63, 83
congressional charter 18, 35, 39
Constantinople, Turkey 34
coordinating efforts 70, 71
Crimean War 23
Cuba 34, 35, 62, 63
current programs 75–83
Curtis, George William 9

D

Davison, Henry P. 49
Delano, Jane 46
democracy 10
Denmark 25
Department of the Army 18
Department of Defense 71
Department of Health and Human
  Services 71
Department of Justice 39
Department of State 8, 39
Department of the Navy 39
Department of the Treasury 8,
  39
Department of War 8, 39
Depression 11, 51–55
disaster relief 30–33, 40, 41
Dunant, Jean-Henry 21–23, 30,
  43

E

Eastland 42
emblem 23, 24, 29, 39

90

O

Operation New Life 65
operational headquarters 67, 69
organ and tissue donations 79
Outpost Service 46, 88

P

patronage 9
peacetime programs 30, 49–51
Pearl Harbor, Hawaii 55
Pendleton Act 10
Philippines 35
president of the United States 8–11, 72
Prussia, 23, 24, 28
Prussian-Danish War 19, 25

R

racial discrimination 13
Reagan, Ronald 12, 83
Red Crescent Societies (see League of Red Cross and . . .)
Red Cross Life Saving Corps 42
Red Cross War Council 45, 49
refugees 45, 58, 61–63, 65
regional headquarters 67
rehabilitation 32
Roosevelt, Franklin D. 54
Roosevelt, Theodore 35, 37, 40
Rough Riders 35
Russia 23, 24, 32
Russo-Turkish War 28

S

St. Louis, Missouri 67
Salvation Army 71
San Francisco earthquake 40, 41
Saxony 24
semigovernmental status 18, 39
separation of powers 8
slavery 13
Spain 24
Spanish-American War 34, 35
spoils system 9, 10
State Department (see Department of State)

street people (see homeless Americans)
Sweden 24
Switzerland 21–24, 28

T

Three Mile Island, Pennsylvania 70
Treasury Department (see Department of the Treasury)
Truman, Harry 60
Tynehead 33

U

Un Souvenir de Solferino 23
United Nations 58, 60
United States 25, 27–29, 39
United States Armed Forces 34
United States Postal Service 63
United States Senate 29
United Way 73, 88

V

Vietnam War 15, 64, 65
volunteers 17, 47, 49–52, 57, 58, 72, 76

W

wagon wheel 67, 68
War Department (see Department of War)
war relief 43–48, 55–58, 59–61, 64–65
Washington, D.C. 37, 67, 78
Washington, George 8
water safety 42, 43
Wilson, Woodrow 45, 48, 49
Workmen's Compensation 41
World War I 43–48, 60
World War II 11, 55–58, 59
Würtemburg 25

Y

Young Men's Christian Associations (YMCAs) 21
youth programs 82